Paul Almasy Paris

Paul Almasy Paris

By Klaus Kleinschmidt
and Axel Schmidt

Prestel

Munich · London · New York

On the cover: Rock 'n' Roll
on the banks of the Seine, 1950s (see p. 51)

Frontispiece: Entrance to the
Chaussée d'Antin Metro station, 1948

Translated from the German
by Stephen Telfer, Edinburgh
Copy-edited by Curt Holtz, Munich

Library of Congress Control Number: 2001093009

Die Deutsche Bibliothek – CIP-Cataloguing-in-
Publication-Data is available

© Prestel Verlag, Munich • London • New York, 2001
of all photos illustrated © Paul Almasy/akg-images

Prestel Verlag • Mandlstrasse 26
80802 Munich
Tel. +49 (89) 3817090; Fax +49 (89) 38170935

4 Bloomsbury Place • WC1A 2QA London
Tel. +44 (020) 7323-5004; Fax +44 (020) 7636-8004

175 Fifth Avenue, Suite 402 • New York, NY 10010
Tel. +1 (212) 995-2720; Fax +1 (212) 995-2733

www.prestel.com

Prestel books are available worldwide. Please
contact your nearest bookseller or one of the
above Prestel offices for details concerning your
local distributor.

Design and typography
by Iris von Hoesslin, Munich
Lithography by Eurocrom 4, Villorba
Printed by Sellier-Druck, Freising
Bound by Conzella, Munich

Printed in Germany on acid-free paper

ISBN 3-7913-2597-3

Contents

Paul Almasy
A Hungarian in Paris

Klaus Kleinschmidt

I do not agree with those who define photography as a "language", but think of it as a script... Don't say photography is a language, but speak about the language of photography.
                                        Paul Almasy

The recent history of photography in Hungary reveals a wealth of great names: Robert Capa, Moholy-Nagy, Martin Munkasci, André Kertész and Stephan Lorant. Newcomers have a hard time of it when they have to be measured against yardsticks like these! So who is Paul Almasy? A new and talented practitioner in photography's pantheon? Certainly he's got more than his fair share of talent, but is he new? When I first met this Hungarian photographer a few years ago, he was no longer young, of course, having been born in 1906. He gave me a compact account of his life that was almost like a time-lapse film: three interviews in a row, as if he wanted to get his massed experiences off his chest. Turning his back on his homeland aged only seventeen, the youngster embarked on an adventurous and incredible life lived out of a suitcase. From Budapest he moved first to Vienna where he studied medicine – for all of one term, as he couldn't bear the smell of chloroform. Lectures in pathology – mostly "bloody" – did their bit to put the visually sensitive Hungarian off the subject. Thereupon he changed subjects and towns. A scion of ancient Hungarian nobility, he moved to Munich where he studied diplomacy. On graduating, life took him to Vevey in Switzerland and then on to Monte Carlo from where he moved again to Paris – where he stayed and is now an old man.

That's Paul Almasy's life in summary. His work is now receiving much wider public attention. It was in 1999 that I gave my first talk in a Wiesbaden gallery about his work. At the time, we – the Archiv für Kunst und Geschichte (AKG) Berlin and Photonet – were showing a small selection of his photographs to mark the publication of the first monograph celebrating this important observer of contemporary life. Jean-Christoph Ammann from Frankfurt's Museum of Modern Art introduced the event in a small room. After years of preparation, the AKG Berlin and Photonet were finally able to let the world in on a secret.

In no time, Mainz-based ZDF, one of Germany's public service television broadcasters, showed a special feature about Almasy's photographs. The first big exhibition of his work followed in Frankfurt's Museum of Modern Art. In what was a promising start, Paul Almasy's photos were hung alongside iconic images by Andy Warhol and Jeff Wall. The response was huge and unanimously positive: national newspapers were enthusiastic in their critiques; reports and features were shown on TV.

Exhibitions in other cities quickly followed on from those in Frankfurt and Mainz, among them one called *Prosa der Welt* (Prose of the World) adjacent to Munich's Haus der Kunst. In the meantime the Anita Neugebauer Gallery in Basel and the Norbert Bunge Gallery in Berlin had shown examples of his work. It would not be long before Almasy was honoured with the most comprehensive retrospective to date at the *Fototage* in Herten; he was also voted *Photography Personality of 2000*. This touring exhibition of more than 107 photographs was next shown at the *Fototage* in the Swiss town of Biel (Museum Pasquart). Yet another more recent venue for it was Budapest's Museum Ernst, an exhibition that drew the Hungarian public's attention to Almasy's life's work. The Regional Museum in the German town of Oldenburg had great success with a special exhibition entitled *Paul Almasy – Hommage à Paris*. Several new bundles of photographs from the AKG's archives were thus added to his collected life's work. These previously unseen works were first put on show in Photonet's galleries. It remains something of a puzzle, however, that the French seem to be unaware of 'their' photographer.

It is something of a coup to be able to introduce this collection of Almasy's Paris photographs. Munich's Prestel Verlag was so taken with the idea of a separate publication that it had no hesitation at all in deciding to publish a book focusing solely on them. It has long been recognised that Paul Almasy is a first-rate observer of contemporary life whom I, in my first monograph on him, unwittingly called a "zaungast der zeitgeschichte" (observer of history). He himself was rather annoyed at the phrase at the time, as he admitted to me in Frankfurt over a dinner with friends. He was many things, he said, but not a rubbernecker prone to stealing surreptitious glances, let alone someone who would photograph without permission! The title of the book was, of course, intended to honour Paul Almasy.

Let's take a closer look at the word 'zaungast'. It means that someone observes events, but does get involved in them. He keeps his distance – not *too* far away, but not right up there either lest he influence events. Robert Capa said: "If your photo is no good, you weren't close enough". This verdict, one that has been understood by generations of photojournalists, loses its decades-old validity when there is too little distance between the photographer and his subject. Because it is only when he keeps a proper distance that the observer can document his era. He closely watches what happens. And the image of an observer is just right here: he is someone looking on, not gawking or being voyeuristic; discreet observation takes the place of a gawk prompted by sheer nosiness. And an onlooker at the sidelines of contemporary life engages with it and bears witness to it with his photographs.

Paul Almasy can look back on a life that has taken him to every country in the world except Mongolia. His career started as a journalist. He has travelled the five continents from north to south and east to west and has crossed all of the world's deserts. He has been everywhere using all kinds of transport: through the jungle on a palanquin, across the Sahara by jeep, across the savannah by bus, through the streets of Saigon in a rickshaw, taken a Skymaster to Tunis and been by sledge to visit the Eskimos. Privative or not, the term *utopia* (Greek for 'no place') denotes a place in the twentieth century, the century of travel.

The constant restlessness that characterizes journalism well suited a man like Almasy, a keen traveller. In 1925 the first Leica came on the market and Almasy soon changed from the written word to the image – not a particularly rare thing in the early days of journalism. Yet the outstanding quality of his reports quickly marked him out as a doubly-gifted man. He had a sharp eye for everything around him. This is how observer's moments arose: Almasy formed his own image of the world during the century he lived through and noted down what he saw.

Whoever talks about "the century" usually means the one just gone, the century of photojournalism and mass media. Let's not forget that certain German-language publications – the *Berliner*, *Münchner* and *Schweizer Illustrirte* – played leading roles in the early days of the then-still-new medium. This was in the 1930s when its pioneers were often self-taught, some of them real war-horses and chancers. Their names were Alfred Eisenstaedt, Robert Capa, Erich Salomon or Walter Bosshard; others were brazen aesthetes like Man Ray, Moholy-Nagy or Martin Munkacsi. There were also self-effacing artists as well as pariahs among them: Werner Bischof, André Kertész, Jacob Tuggener or, among the less shy, Cartier-Bresson and Gisèle Freund. It was truly the era of the magazine – and time for the photojournalist to make his entrance. This was the era when Paul Almasy shaped our view of the world. As a reporter on the flagship of Swiss magazines he took on the role of all-rounder. He felt at ease wherever he was in the world. The appetite of people back home for images from across the globe, their curiosity about life in distant places, was *huge*. With their work, photojournalists made their way into people's living rooms for the first time. Gripping articles meant that magazines rolled off the presses in astronomical numbers. Just as it is difficult to conceive of Almasy's work without these magazines, the magazines themselves would have been all the poorer without his sharp eye.

Ingrid Bergman at a Hungarian wedding, 1952

Almasy travelled back and forth between Monte Carlo and Paris during the war years and soon wanted to live in France. Jules Verne helped him along, writing that Almasy wanted to live "here, here and only here". The *grande nation* did not welcome him with open arms, however, but tolerated his presence. In the 1950s, his work for organizations like WHO, UNESCO and UNICEF increased in importance and for forty years Almasy travelled the world in their service. His travels resulted in social reportage that unobtrusively related events as they unfolded, his articles capturing the essence of distant cultures in words and pictures. This globe-trotter *par excellence* had by then long been in possession of a special U.N. permit allowing him unlimited entry to countries and was by now enjoying the privileges of a diplomat. Almasy received French citizenship in 1956: the citizen of the world was now a citizen of France with Paris as his chosen home and the airport he set out from to conquer the world.

And today? For quite a few years now, Paul Almasy has led a secluded life in Auteuil le Roi, a small village not far from Paris, and it was there that we first met. I was then on the road all the time in my capacity as photography critic for some big magazines and newspapers and was, of course, keen to meet this long-forgotten Nestor of photojournalism. The AKG arranged a meeting. Almasy was proud to show me his collection that – this much I suspect – is unique in the history of photography. His estate, a rare wealth of text and images, has now been transferred, still during his lifetime, to the care of the AKG in Berlin. A start has been made and now almost half of his work has been catalogued by legend, key word and reference number. According to strict criteria, certain examples of his work were certified as masterprints and signed by Almasy for a small circle of curators and collectors. It was, in fact, the AKG under Justus Goepel that recognized the outstanding quality of Almasy's photographic collection back in 1995. It acquired his complete black and white oeuvre and has since been cataloguing and maintaining his estate.

And so it was that one day I caught a train from Paris' Montparnasse station to go and see Paul Almasy. Somewhere, at the edge of the city, a station alongside two empty tracks appeared as if out of nowhere. There wasn't a soul to be seen on the platforms, but Elina Almasy, my host's young wife, who had been described to me earlier, waved to me, gesturing me to come. Her car was parked around the corner. A high-spirited seventy-year-old, she made the engine roar. We set off. It was only a short drive to the house, she reassured me. We drove along winding country roads before, at long last, a sign announcing the village appeared before us. The Renault bumped across a few metres of cobblestones straight into the Grande Rue where Almasy and his wife live.

A key grated in the lock of the weathered wooden door that opened onto the courtyard. It opened reluctantly and promptly stuck. Madame Almasy got physical: after a sharp jolt, the old door opened grudgingly. A friendly Labrador bounded towards me across a courtyard covered in coarse gravel. Pruned alder trees lined the garden that was raised above the level of the courtyard. A rough stone wall enclosed the whole property. In front of it, there was an unkempt and picturesque garden that was strangely beautiful. To the left and right surrounding the courtyard on either side were the living quarters of dressed stone. The one on the right, probably the working quarters at one time, housed the wealth of photographs that I was soon to see.

Paul Almasy was making his way down a flight of stone steps at the side of the house. He was a bit unsteady on his feet, which didn't surprise me. Even then he was just short of what was a ripe old age. He is now almost 100 years old, a span of time that he has not experienced passively. At the start of his career, his photographs recorded history in the making. When he was better known, he made history himself – photographic history. Certain moments of great intensity were positively 'frozen' in time and the spirit of the early days seemed to come alive. There are times when history is encapsulated in a single gesture, times when Almasy practically had to 'disappear'. How did he do it? Discretion provided his favourite cloak of invisibility. But really, the 'decisive moment' of a Cartier-Bresson, the emotiveness of an up-front Robert Capa wasn't Almasy's style at all. He was not interested in stylised compositions or theatricality; his aim was 'honesty made visible'.

So here he was: tall, straight as a die, a slightly furrowed brow, his eyebrows pointing sharply upwards as if he constantly wanted to ask questions. This was the face of someone who had seen a lot: his eyes looked alert and flashed mischievously. And then there were his big, heavy hands that had lost none of their power. They alone could tell his life's story. On one of his wrists, he wore a mechanical chronograph. Exact timing and time itself had been important to him since the 1930s when he began his nomadic life. As a young journalist, he believed that time was money; as an old man, he knows that time is something that passes.

The weather was unpleasant that morning. Paul Almasy walked up the steps into the living room that was warmed by a real fire whose flames danced as a result of the gust of wind that blew into the room with that day's visitor. It was a perishingly cold March day, in fact. We went upstairs to his office on the first floor. Almasy walked across to a cupboard and gently removed his camera from a drawer. He removed the protective brass caps from the two-eyed Rollei. "I took almost all my photographs using this camera", he said. At first, he worked using a Leica, then later a Rollei. How many times must he have pressed the shutter release on his camera? And how often must he have hesitated before doing so, despite his initial impulse? What scenes did he close his eyes to? We don't know but his photographs, the images he captured on film, can tell us. And they certainly have a lot to say.

Over the course of sixty years, Almasy the photographer, journalist and trained political scientist worked tirelessly on his "archive of the world". A recipient of numerous photography awards and a 'Chevallier de l'Ordre du Mérite', Almasy was called to the Sorbonne as a visiting lecturer in his old age and his career took on a new dimension. But his main focus remains his work on the archive, a cultural treasure of the very first order that the multilingual photojournalist has organised meticulously according to countries and subject matter. The material, unique in its simplicity, is now finally coming to the attention of a

On the aircraft carrier Midway, 1952

wider public. Until now it has mainly been the preserve of *cognoscenti* who themselves probably only knew certain aspects of Almasy's wide-ranging work.

Paul Almasy met several public figures including government leaders and artists. Most of them were creators like himself, pioneers in some way or, like him, witnesses to their age. He mixed in bohemian circles and high society alike and captured on film the parties and rituals of both. He knew Otto von Habsburg and the Baron de Rothschild. He visited President Eisenhower as well as Begin, Khrushchev, de Gaulle, Evita Peron, Mussolini and, later, Mitterrand or Reza Shah. As a novice reporter he met Hitler during an interview with Rosenberg in the 'Braunes Haus'. And all the while, exotic kings, heads of state and dictators were described in his press columns that the world used to form its images of distant cultures. In his writing, he avoided all pretension. For Almasy, the main aim of photojournalism was to inform. It isn't, of course, as prosaic as that: his work is spellbinding to a rare degree.

To this day, Almasy, the photographer, despises vain poses. His viewfinder hardly ever captured affectation on film. Whoever insisted on pleasing him was quickly dropped as a subject: he really was *not* looking for 'models'. And it is this objective 'prose of looking' of his that makes this photojournalist with an ability to empathize a lucky find indeed. Whether he found himself in the throng of a city or the South American jungle, this unwilling aesthete always wanted to see 'ordinary' people and wanted to know how they lived. He may not have shared the same fate as them, but he did join them at a discreet distance. To this day he rejects intent behind composition. Such vanity is anathema to him. Almasy believes that too much aesthetic sense is something that hardly becomes pioneers of the genre. Yet anyone looking at his photographs cannot fail to be captivated by their beauty. "I am not a photographer", he objected to reporters from Munich's *Süddeutsche Zeitung*. "Sorry", they replied, "we just think your photos are lovely".

Paul Almasy's is a multifaceted oeuvre encompassing the rice harvest in Indonesia, nomads in the Sahara, midwives in the Sudan, a shipyard in Sakai, mentally-ill patients in Burundi, the slums of Rio, a remote petrol station in the desert, Goethe's ruined house, a Zulu woman walking along a pavement – the list of subjects is almost endless. The archive is estimated to contain 120,000 photographs that are little known outside of Germany. Visit the AKG in Berlin, where the estate is now held, and wherever you turn you'll come across boxes full to overflowing with photos from around the world and in between them reports and tickets that the photographer had collected over the years. Here you can rummage through an archive that in scope and significance equals Albert Kahn's Archive of the Planet. The difference here is that the archivist, collector, curator and creator of the whole thing was one and the same man. It pleased the aged Almasy to hear that an aura of high art now surrounds his collection but he still insists vigorously that the truthfulness of the information it conveys is what matters to him.

"When I took a photograph, I never crouched down like a cat about to pounce on its prey. Lots of photojournalists do, but I think it's just silly. I never attacked with my camera." Among photographers, Paul Almasy is, in fact, something of a blue-blooded street-worker. Like Lewis Hine, Dorothea Lange or Walker Evans before him, Almasy was interested in the social conditions experienced by the rich and the poor of the world. As a working photojournalist, he was completely unaware of his predecessors and it was not until his professorship that he was able to study them in detail. He can now appreciate the commitment of Roy Stryker, say, the photographer who, on behalf of the Farm Security Administration (FSA), recorded the poverty and hunger of farm labourers in the American Midwest. Almasy, the guest lecturer at the Sorbonne, not only knows the FSA photographers by name; with them he shares the same profession and the same era.

In his old age, Almasy devotes time to his archive, a treasure of the highest order that needs to be carefully maintained and organised. Interest in Almasy's work increased steadily throughout the 1990s, a time when demand on the European art market for the work of the trailblazers of photojournalism started to grow. Demand for the time being is still American-driven and collectors like Sam Wagstaff take the credit for it. Almasy, a typical outsider and self-taught man with no advocates and not a member of any school, escaped the attention of photography's great 'scouts' and the backers of a modern press, Hans

Finsler, Arnold Kübler, Stephan Lorant and Edward Steichen, who in the '30s, '40s and '50s were on the look-out for up-and-coming talent.

While Almasy's fellow Hungarians have long known of Brassai, Capa, Kertész and Moholy-Nagy, the era of reportage knows very little about him. Such a discrepancy is almost absurd because Almasy's reportages describe our emergence into the media age. It is thanks to people like him, from among the ranks of pioneers, that the photo-essay became established in Europe in the '50s. Almasy's visual style is not spectacular, but it does impress itself on the mind. Maybe that is why he wasn't carried along by the tide of time? His colleagues, such as his competitors at Magnum, knew how to sell themselves.

New treasures from last century's Aladdin's cave of photography are now coming to light with the result that one cannot help but mention the photographer, who doggedly maintains he isn't one, in the same breath as Erich Salomon and Walter Bosshardt, or place him in his significance as a witness to contemporary events alongside Gisèle Freund, Marc Riboud or Henri Cartier-Bresson and regard him as one of the pre-eminent chroniclers of the twentieth century. The striking work of this Hungarian photographer has a long way to go yet before it is exhausted.

The famous scholars of antiquity – from Pliny to Plutarch – often thought of a universal history of mankind and dreamt about writing it. Like many geniuses before him, Denis Diderot had the same thought in the eighteenth century. Yet it was inevitable that those who wielded the quill would fail in view of the magnitude of the task. When the technology of photography was discovered in 1839, the same desire was again felt strongly. To have the courage to attempt to create a world consciousness, an 'archive' of the planet, using photography was an idea rooted in the Utopianism of the early Industrial Revolution and it still gripped world spirits in modern times. Even in more recent times, there has been no lack of less ambitious attempts or models: think of Edward Steichen's mammoth photography show that this font of wisdom about modern photographic imagery concluded with his 1955 project *Family of Man*, a title that could also be applied to Almasy's agenda which took him on yet more journeys to ever more remote locations. August Sanders' unfinished

Filling station in Algeria, 1963

Zulu woman, 1953

Midwifes in Sudan, 1963

Man in the 20th Century also belongs to this illustrious circle, of course. It is in the nature of such projects that they remain fragments.

Neither did Albert Kahn's genial idea to create a worldwide 'archive of the planet' using autochromes, in which every bit of the Earth was to be included, escape him – a Parisian by choice. In an off-print of a lecture that Almasy gave at the Sorbonne in the 1980s, we find an intentional trail back to Kahn: "Special mention must be made of the work of a group of photographers working for the banker Albert Kahn. His photographers visited every country in the world to create the archive. Their reports were not intended for publication in the press, but because of their subject matter – people's lives, activities and the difficulties they faced – they were clearly journalistic in character."

Just as Albert Kahn (1860–1940) left Alsace for Paris, Almasy landed in the French capital, too. In contrast to the banker who was able to leave his origins behind him, and with his diamond mines became France's richest man and rapidly gained status and influence, Almasy remained true to himself and his love of adventure – a tactful observer who at no point was interested in mere participation. While the wealthy banker, who as a young student was tutored privately by Bergson, had others 'experience' for him, Almasy remained eager to do his own experiencing well into his old age. He did not have such 'operators', men sent out into the world by Kahn in his place. Almasy single-mindedly built up his archive that makes no claim to be global in scale, and it simply grows with the years – so much so that its panorama of foreign countries and their customs has become quite unique.

Almasy was resolute in his view of the syntax of photographs: "I do not agree with those who define photography as a 'language', but think of it as a script... Don't say photography is a language, but speak about the language of photography". Roland Barthes, in contrast, in his book *Camera Lucida: Reflections on Photography* recalls that the editors of *Life* rejected Kertész's photos outright when he arrived in New York in 1937 because they allegedly 'said too much', prompted too much thought and contained too much meaning, undermining the magazine's intention. The magazine photographer, it was said, was seeking affirmation and personified public discourse indiscriminately. Barthes: "But photography is basically always subversive, not when people find it repugnant or are horrified by it, or when it denounces something, but when it makes people think."

Almasy's style does not follow fashion. It is derived from a sense of high-minded enlightenment that he, a student of politics versed in diplomacy – embraced with his camera, a stance that he retains for all time and never really changes. This self-taught photographer views things very much from a political viewpoint. Almasy has none of the creative 'phases' or 'periods' found throughout the early and late work of Werner Bischof or Robert Frank. Into his old age, he shoots his photos in a stylistically 'timeless' fashion – although they are clearly imbued with the *Zeitgeist*, albeit in a way that is different from the 'casual' by the likes of Robert Doisneau or Jacques Lartigue. And whoever takes a closer look at his work will see that social is-

sues are always the focus of his attention. There's no place here for the perfect picture, no matter how attractive it may look.

Even at the age of eighty Almasy travelled around the world, although he has now long tired of travel. This observer now faces his own eventide. He rummaged in a bundle of photos and pulled out a few at random: "Heavens! Le Pen, but in his young days." There's almost regret in the voice of a man who has travelled to the furthermost corners of the earth and knows them like the back of his hand – sorrow at lost time.

A little nostalgia overcame this doyen of photojournalism as he leaned back in his chair. One particular image keeps coming back to him, he said. He closed his eyes, seeing it in front of him as if it was yesterday. It took him back to his childhood in Hungary: a country village called Tahitótfalu overlooking the Danube, forty kilometres north of Budapest. Almasy knew every field, meadow and tree. It was here on his mother's farm that he had his first contact with the bohemian life, where artists and singers came and went; this was the idyll of Paul Almasy's youth and this is what he still yearns for.

Almasy and photography – an unusually long-lasting love, especially since it hasn't waned yet. Was it his passion? Almasy's reply to this was surprisingly succinct and prosaic: "No, I simply had to do it. It was always chance that decided everything. I never did the searching; my camera did. I was just the finder and what I found I photographed." True to his maxim, Almasy strolled through our century. "Witness to our century" – this too eagerly used phrase truly does apply to him. Glancing at the last photograph, his face brightened again: "Heavens, Baron de Rothschild!" The memory is concluded with a sigh. "The atmosphere was always good – just like his wines." The old man's thoughts strayed back to his youth again. In a pensive moment he suddenly admitted why he left home back then, what prompted him to lead a unique life that is now nearing its end: "Life at home was miserable. I didn't want to stay, so I left."

Brick production in Pakistan, 1950

Transporting coal in India, 1962

Paul Almasy, Paris:
The City and the Archive

Axel Schmidt

1. Texts of the City

You read the leaflets catalogues posters
that sing at the top of their voices
That's this morning's poetry and for prose
there are the newspapers   Guillaume Apollinaire, *Zone*[1]

"I am not a photographer. I am a journalist and photo-journalist. I combine these two activities and in my work use two different styles: a written one and a pictorial one. At the start of my career I was merely a journalist, and when I was asked to add pictures to my articles, I hadn't the least clue about photography. When I began to familiarize myself with its techniques, I discovered that when I performed these two activities together, I was practising one and the same profession."[2]

With his background in writing, Paul Almasy never thought twice about photographing writing, anything legible or signs. Time and again in his work we find inscriptions, slogans, posters, signs and even traffic signs. People reading and writing or billposters at work also repeatedly attracted his attention.[3] Indeed, it was his eye for the literal that launched the start of his career as a photographer. Almasy had worked as a journalist since 1929 and in 1935 received his first commission from the *Berliner Illustrirte Zeitung* for an illustrated article. He was to file a report on the Finnish team's preparations for the Winter Olympic Games in 1936. When Almasy returned from the job, his editor was greatly taken with the way he had captured the bitter cold on film: Almasy had simply photographed a thermometer. From then on, the legibility of the world was always one of his subjects.

Yet Almasy, who as a young journalist had interviewed Mussolini and met Hitler in the 'Braunes Haus', did not grasp the career opportunity available to him in Berlin on the eve of World War II. Instead he became a correspondent for the *Schweizer Illustrirte Zeitung* and moved to Monaco. He was there when it was shelled and photographed

the action. He took many photographs in the occupied and non-occupied zones of France. In a Paris occupied by German troops, a man removes posters put up by the defeated French army; conspicuous black and white signposts in front of the opera give directions in German for the *Wehrmacht* (army). It was there in May 1945 that Almasy photographed jubilant Parisians carrying a picture of Winston Churchill. And the newspaper headlines that day read: "It's over!", "Nazi Germany defeated!". Paris belonged to the French again and Paul Almasy made it his home.

After the liberation, Almasy settled in Paris and opened an office where a secretary started working for him in September 1945. His earliest article about the city was written back in 1936. Starting with his first commission from the *Berliner Illustrirte Zeitung*, Almasy numbered his articles consecutively; by the end of his career he had reached number 1,562. "Ça c'est Paris!" was his twenty-ninth reportage. Its photos show the Paris everyone knows: the Sacré-Cœur, the *Grands Boulevards*, Chanel mannequins, a typical bistro... Yet his critical eye was more searching. "This 'capital of the world'", Almasy noted, "is no longer the city of ostentatious luxury, of proverbial vice (...), but (...) rather is an edgy metropolis struggling with life..." and he concluded: "One question will always go unanswered: is Paris a city of the past, the present or the future?"[4]

For more than fifty years, Almasy would follow the developments and sweeping changes affecting one of the twentieth century's most captivating cities. Only after that length of time would he retire to the country.

Shots for his next article showed a "City of the Future" complete with skyscrapers – albeit only in blueprints and as models. "This man wants to transform New York! The famous architect Le Corbusier in his office".[5] The monumentalism of the 1937 Paris International Exposition, with the pavilions of the Soviet Union and Nazi Germany, seemed not to have made a lasting impression on Almasy who, with a quite different phenomenon in mind, only a short while later talked about a "new era of civilisation".[6] His article on "The Age of the Petrol Can" contrasted urban utopias, whether of the modern age, whether of totalitarianism, with a very real phenomenon: the world's slums and shantytowns, known as *bidonville* in French. "Today both in Asia and Africa there are whole villages made of empty petrol cans. Besides the dwellings, there is hardly a household object that is not made of these metal cans."[7] Almasy's horizon was already a global one, his view having been shaped by Italy, Germany, Belgium, The Netherlands, Great Britain, Yugoslavia, Bulgaria, Romania, Albania, Turkey, several Latin American countries, Finland, the Sahara, Togo, Morocco, Niger, Benin, Greece, Libya, The Lebanon, Syria, Iraq, the Baltic States, Cameroon, the Comoros, the Ivory Coast, Djibouti, Zanzibar, Madagascar, Mozambique, South Africa, Namibia, Palestine, Aden,

End of the war, 1945

Somalia, and the Arabian States under British mandate. Almasy, a native Hungarian, had visited all those countries in the first ten years of his career before World War II, an event that for him mainly meant the postponement of further journeys to distant places. He was an accredited correspondent for the Swiss press covering France, Germany, Belgium and The Netherlands at *Wehrmacht* and German press offices.

It was in 1946/47 that Almasy was able to resume his travels beyond the borders of Europe and he filed reports from the Middle East, Algeria, Egypt, Greece, Nubia, and Mali. The map of the world had changed. During the 1946 Paris Peace Conference, he considered the new balance of power and its immediate consequences. "It is possible that the role of emigration from European countries has never been so complicated or ambiguous as now", he wrote in a major article about "France as a Place of Asylum". To fulfil its political obligations, while at the same time meeting its need for workers, France had agreed to take in 200,000 displaced persons in 1947/48.[8] Almasy was particularly interested in refugees from Central and Eastern Europe as he had spent his childhood and youth in Hungary, then still part of the Austro-Hungarian Empire, that Eastern European, multiracial state which disappeared off the map at the end of World War I.

After World War II, his country came under Soviet influence that was further consolidated by the suppression of the Hungarian Revolution of 1956 – the year Almasy became a French citizen. He had left his homeland of his own accord in 1924. He made the issues of emigration and cosmopolitanism very much his own – which is unsurprising considering his roots in a people from the steppes of Asia, his Bavarian grandmother, his study of political science at Vienna, Munich and Heidelberg, and considering that the start of his career was as a journalist in Rome and, not least, that he had already travelled abroad widely. His article entitled "Second Home Paris"[9] focused on women from five continents. Almasy mentioned "the French capital's unique capacity to assimilate" that in no time at all makes *Parisiennes* of foreign women, then mostly Poles and Italians. It was a long-established tradition, in fact. Even during the *Ancien Régime*, the 'nation' and citizenship were defined politically, not in terms of one's origins.[10] Throughout the whole of the nineteenth century right up until the middle of the twentieth century, France absorbed more immigrants than any other country in Europe.[11] From the time of the French Revolution, Paris never ceased to be a haven for the victims of political persecution, among them Germans fleeing the failed revolution of 1848 and Poles in the nineteenth century. The Russian political refugees who arrived in waves before and after the October Revolution had made Paris the "political capital of Russian émigrés",[12] as Saskia Sassen put it. Almasy wrote some articles about the Russian community and described how the various waves of immigrants assimilated into it.[13]

Paris had likewise become an important centre of Jewish life. Like the United States, Amsterdam, Vienna and (formerly) Berlin, Paris, since the end of the nineteenth century, attracted many Jews fleeing anti-Semitism and pogroms in Eastern Europe.[14] Almasy took large numbers

of shots in the Jewish quarter of Paris in the post-war years, examining the stories of a number of individuals.

In the 1920s and '30s, they were followed by refugees fleeing the totalitarian regimes of Mussolini, Hitler and Franco. There were hundreds of thousands of Spaniards living in France after the end of the Spanish Civil War and Almasy, interested in social and political issues from the start of his career, investigated their often harsh circumstances.[15]

It was not only for political reasons that immigrants were allowed into France, however. As already mentioned above, there was a huge shortage of labour after the war – so much so that France even made efforts to obtain workers from its erstwhile wartime enemy. "France suggested to the Allies that it was willing to accept further contingents of displaced persons from Germany on condition that the same number of German workers could be recruited in addition",[16] Almasy wrote in 1947 in his above-mentioned article. That alone tells us how important immigration was for a country whose population had been stagnating since the turn of the century. Of the countries of Europe, France had already suffered the greatest losses in terms of men killed and disabled during World War I. If France wanted to develop from an agrarian country into a modern industrialized nation, immigration had to be actively promoted for demographic and economic reasons.[17] Indeed, it was the number of incoming refugees and immigrant workers, besides the general exodus from the country to the towns since the end of World War II, that had slowed the decline, since 1921, of the population of Paris. The Allies nevertheless rejected the French request in 1947 out of consideration for Germany's own reconstruction.

The largest contingent of immigrant workers in twentieth-century France was the Portuguese (in the nineteenth century it had still been Italians). The majority of these workers were employed in the building industry. Without them, the modernization of Paris, begun in the 1950s, could not have been completed. "There are currently 150,000 Portuguese workers in France, most of whom have come here legally over the past 20 years – in other words, since the end of the war",[18] Almasy wrote in the 1960s. "The greatest episode ever of trafficking in human beings has been going at full swing for the past three years between Portugal and France. Around 25,000

Jacqueline Rothhahn, his secretary, 1950s   Almasy with his Leica, 1950s

Portuguese workers have left their homeland illegally, crossed Spain furtively and have been smuggled into France across the Pyrenees."[19] Almasy described the stories of several individuals and instances of illegal border crossing into France. He photographed Portuguese workers on their way to work, on building sites, on their way back home and in one of the largest colonies of Portuguese workers: Champigny-sur-Marne, situated beyond the Paris city boundary. This was home to 10,000 people living in shacks and tiny 'houses' they had built themselves without official permission. There was no water supply, no sewerage system, and no refuse collection.

While the Portuguese used stone to build their accommodation, the shacks erected by North African immigrants, as photographed by Almasy in Nanterre, often consisted only of planks of wood, corrugated iron and cardboard. For people from the former French colonies – Algeria, Morocco, Tunisia – France was and still is the first choice when they emigrate.[20] Especially the French car industry and iron foundries depended on this particular group of immigrants. Owing to the high rents and the serious housing shortage in Paris itself, the settlements skirting the city continued to grow unabated. "Several of these makeshift settlements were similar to the *bidonvilles* of Rabat, Casablanca and other North African cities."[21]

Two decades after Almasy first used the term *bidonville* in an article – he even left it untranslated in a German text – he again, in 1954 united this urban extreme in one image. His "Two sides of the hill" was shot in Rio de Janeiro and shows Copacabana, where the wealthy live in modern homes with a sea view, and the *favelas* of Morro dos Cabritos, the shanty town inhabited by the poor on the landward side. In 1976, Almasy was awarded first prize for this photograph at the United Nations Conference on Human Settlements, Habitat, in Vancouver. The problems illustrated by his photograph have since worsened throughout the world and continue to grow. The increasing rate of urbanisation will be one of the twenty-first century's great phenomena.

The dividing line between the First and the Third World that Almasy had crossed so often was also found within Paris: it ran between the stone façades of the city centre and the *banlieue*, the suburbs. Almasy argued that the Paris police did not know the exact number of North Africans living in the city. France had already brought in Algerian workers after World War I and their numbers

had risen sharply. "After 1933 the numbers of incoming North Africans rose year after year, and especially the numbers coming from Algeria because the former colony was administratively the equivalent of a *Département* of the mother country, which means that the Arabs from Algeria can readily travel to Paris without a passport or special permit and settle there just as a resident of any other French *Département* can do."[22] "Couscous, Arabic music and belly dancers: that's about the sum of what a visitor to Paris sees and learns about the North Africans. The atmosphere in Arab night spots in the Latin Quarter reveals nothing of the seriousness of the problems created for Paris by the presence in the city of around 180,000 North Africans",[23] Almasy wrote.

It was mainly in the 1950s that the myth of Paris arose, the one that to this day shapes the tourist image of the city. Paris came through World War II having suffered almost no major damage and again became a magnet for people from across the world. Post-war Paris re-established itself as the capital of art thanks to its young artists and those returning from exile. During Almasy's visits to Paris – they must be called 'visits' because he was often on the road for nine months of the year – he created a kaleidoscope of the city's cultural life. Among the many figures whose portrait he took were such famous names as Alberto Giacometti, Bernard Buffet, Georges Mathieu, Foujita, Man Ray, Ossip Zadkine, Colette, Jacques Prévert, André Breton, Boris Vian, Louis Aragon, Jean-Paul Sartre and Jean Cocteau.

Almasy's archive grew over the years to include series of images of Paris: its buildings, streets and arcades, squares, restaurants and cafés, ordinary folk going about their everyday business. Just as he photographed the world that he saw independently of his articles, so, too, did he photograph Paris. Sometimes we find the odd article by Almasy that evoked the myth of Paris – "Mannequins", "French Cancan", "Tour Eiffel", "An Evening in the Latin Quarter", "A Night in Montmartre"[24] – but he was never content with surface appearances. He wrote about espionage in the fashion world,[25] took photographs in the Métro and the sewers – and in the catacombs where the bones of thousands of deceased Parisians lie stacked – and rather than transfigure the city's youth, he considerd the large number of so-called "*jeunes isolés*",[26] youngsters who have no-one to look after them and who must get on with their lives in the city alone. He produced two series of photographs: "The Life of Youth" and "Youth without Ideals". They showed young Parisians being trained on-the-job and in their spare time in bars, cafés and at dances. Almasy photographed working-class yobs in their "*blousons noirs*"[27] and the scholarly types of the existentialist era in jazz bars. In 1968, two years before he himself started lecturing, he was present when the student revolts erupted. One of his loveliest photographs shows a group of four students in front of the Sorbonne; one of them is reading a copy of the *Internationale Situationiste* and posters of Marx, Lenin and Mao are seen on pillars in the background.

Almasy was also the photographer of the era of decolonization and post-colonialism. The end of World War II for France meant the start of a further sixteen years of war in its colonies. While Paris recovered from the occupation

Portuguese immigrant workers, 1963

and enjoyed the spectacles of its music halls and revues, striptease, jazz and rock 'n' roll, Vietnam, Laos and Cambodia in former French Indochina, and Tunisia, Morocco and Algeria in North Africa asserted their independence from France. Less dramatic was the loss of the black African colonies. "We have decided to take our independence" stated a photograph taken by Almasy in Morocco. Starting in the 1950s, the signs of the break-up of the French colonies were obvious: "You were the past. We are the future." – as photographed by Almasy in Algeria. The symbolism of the photo is further heightened when two young local lads prepare to climb up to the writing. After the defeat at Dien Bien Phu in 1954 and the loss of Indochina, the war in Algeria from 1954 to 1962 became a political, military and economic endurance test that unnerved and divided the whole nation. The position of the French in Algeria was difficult, as was that of Algerian immigrants in France.

"Not so very long ago, the earth numbered two thousand million inhabitants: five hundred million men, and one thousand five hundred million natives",[28] wrote Jean-Paul Sartre in his 1961 preface to Frantz Fanon's *The Wretched of the Earth*. His assessment of Eurocentric thinking was harsh. "This fat, pale continent ends by falling into what Fanon rightly calls narcissism. Cocteau became irritated with Paris – 'that city which talks about itself the whole time'. Is Europe any different?"[29] "Europe is springing leaks everywhere." Sartre found at the time and asked "What then has happened? It simply is that in the past we made history and now it is being made of us. The ratio of forces has been inverted;...".[30] "Paris 2.567 km" says a signpost in the Algerian oilfield of Hassi Messaoud as photographed by Almasy. "Paris 12.672 km" is the distance from a crossroads in Dong Dang, Vietnam. The signposts that once showed the direction to the centre of power now showed the direction of the retreat. In 1950 Almasy joined a family returning to Paris from Vietnam. One million *pieds noirs*, French settlers in Algeria, some of whom had lived there for generations, left the country after the end of the war of independence and Almasy considered their attempts to settle back in France.[31] In all, two million French citizens returned from overseas.[32] With the tricolore of France having been struck, a sign in Algiers read: "Algerians! Whiteness and cleanliness are the symbols of Islam!" An exodus of Jews started from Algeria and Morocco. Almasy wrote an article about their arrival in emergency accommodation in Marseille and examined their integration in Paris.

In the 1950s Paul Almasy started to work for various subsidiary organisations of the U.N.: UNESCO, WHO, IAO and FAO. UNESCO's newly built headquarters was then the flagship of contemporary architecture in the French capital. The shots that Almasy took for these organizations illustrate how modernism came to be so widespread. With Western rationalism, using the grid and statistics, an attempt was made to combat the shortcomings of the decolonized world with its hybrid structures. (One of Almasy's frequently published photos show men sitting on wooden planks being lowered down the side of a modern high-rise in Islamabad so that they could give the building a painted First World appearance using Third

Quartier Nordafricain at Nanterre, 1960   Two sides of the hill, Rio de Janeiro, 1954

World means. In *Black Skin, White Masks*[33] Frantz Fanon described this as a psychological phenomenon of colonized people). In this context, Almasy was always aware of the limitations of photography. There is an overlap between what a photograph can show, and between what can be verified using statistics (which so often feature in Almasy's texts) and what can be described in words. While many photojournalists from Almasy's generation, who emerged from World War II as the only heroes, rushed off immediately to new conflicts, Almasy dealt with crises that were much less conspicuous – even if they did cause greater losses.

The great problems facing humanity – clearly demonstrated in the former colonies in the form of hunger, poor nutrition, drought, lack of water supplies and the repercussions for farming, health and the battle against illness, child mortality, illiteracy, child labour and generally the unsatisfactory levels of education of the people there – have always been Almasy's main issues. Almasy, who first started to study medicine before changing to political science, has always been open to the world and to others. Even at the age of eighty, he was photographing people having an Aids test done!

Once France lost its colonies, Paris began to focus increasingly on its periphery. Having developed over centuries, the centralist structures that converged on Paris tested the city and the Ile-de-France to their limits through the huge developments that took place since the end of World War II. Public transport, the roads and the housing market, too, were unable to cope with the increase in population. "The French generally, and the Parisians in particular, lived in holes, there's no other word for it", wrote Bernard Marrey in retrospect in the 1990s in *Paris perdu. Quarante ans de boueversement de la ville*.[34]

That Paris was able to maintain its identity for decades, at least to the outside, while other capital cities were expanding and changing in character, was not least due to the fact that it retained its ancient city boundaries. Beyond them, however, in the suburbs and in peripheral areas, huge changes had been taking place.

When Almasy first arrived in Paris in the '30s, it still ranked among the world's ten largest cities, of which five were European, two American and three Asian. The city proper had almost three million inhabitants and around five million lived in the Greater Paris area. When he retired at the end of the '80s, the number of Parisians had fallen steadily to just over two million. In the Greater Paris area, however, the number of inhabitants had doubled to ten million. As traditional industries closed down, old, established populations largely moved out of the centre where a process of gentrification began.

What is now the ring road around Paris used to be the start of the 'zone'. "Zone is the Greek word for strip, tract, neither town nor country, another place that does not exist in lists of dwelling places and localities",[35] writes Jean-François Lyotard in his article of that name. Almasy often visited this 'non-place' and reflected on the marginalized people living there. "It was mostly North Africans who lived in the 'zone'", he writes – and like *bidonville* he also uses that word in his German article. The 'zone' was also where the Gypsies camped. Like no other people, the Gypsies in various countries were for decades the object of Almasy's interest and sympathy.[36] At the start of the '60s, work began on demolishing the 'zone', a "symbol of the social wrongs that France had long suffered in the first half of the twentieth century".[37] Almasy recorded the changes: while Gypsies camp in the foreground and the *bidonvilles* are torn down, the first tower blocks can be seen rising in the background.

Fifty articles later, Almasy, in "This is the Paris of Tomorrow",[38] considered the "huge development plan for Paris and the region's general reorganization". Its realization in the city centre, 'decentralization' and 'decongestion' being its key concepts, was to surpass even Baron Haussmann's remodelling in the nineteenth century. The suburbs were to be redeveloped; five *Villes nouvelles* were to be created at a distance of some 15–30 km from the centre. People were to be able to live, work, meet their daily needs, be educated and spend their free time there. This urban blueprint did not envisage a mere extension of the city's traditional boundaries. The intention was rather what Lyotard calls "a philosophy of 'being all together in the world', something very different from the metaphysics of metropolises".[39]

Almasy followed up "This is the Paris of Tomorrow" a short while later by taking a critical look at modern architecture in an article headlined "Artificial Towns". "Are these towns with no past towns with no future?"[40] Using as examples Brasilia, Mourenx in France, Dunapentele in Hungary, Wolfsburg in Germany and Vällingby in Sweden,

and backed up with the findings of surveys among their residents, Almasy, tactful as ever, noted that the most advanced urban projects of their day "give rise to a less happy social and psychological climate among their residents". In the end, modernism is also a story of loss. Lyotard calls the suburbs places of "lamentation",[41] Baudrillard talks of "hate"[42] and the sociologists around Pierre Bourdieu go there in search of the "world's misery".[43]

Back to the city centre. When it was realised that the centre of Paris had been neglected in favour of outlying areas, a process was started that Almasy discussed in his article "The Face of Paris is Changing". "Accused of being Europe's most antiquated capital, the city has now enthusiastically embarked upon a process of rejuvenation."[44] The UNESCO building (1955–58), La Défense (starting in 1958), the Maison de la Radio (1963), the campus at Jussieu for 70,000 students (1965), Montparnasse Tower and Station (1973), Les Halles (1973–79) and the Pompidou Centre (1976–77) are only the most striking instances of modernization in the city. Almasy followed all these developments as a photojournalist, later in more detail. "In every part of town and almost in every street, old buildings are disappearing and new ones are going up from one day to the next."[45] "The historic city of Paris was faced with attacks from within",[46] wrote Philippe Vergne in the mid-'90s about the Paris that had disappeared. By this time Almasy had retired to his home in the country. And yet Paris is still Paris – and has paid the price the Dutch architect and theorist Rem Koolhaas said it would pay. "In the past fifteen years, Paris has become a sort of super Paris, almost a caricature of itself – a dazzling, historic, well-maintained city. Behind its façades a ruthless, but unseen, process of modernization has taken place, yet it is becoming increasingly difficult to change its identity. Paris is a prisoner of its identity, its own myth."[47]

For fifty years, Almasy photographed the visible and described the invisible in Paris. "Paris Behind Closed Doors" is the title of one of his early articles about the city. Almasy knows the myth and the reality of Paris because he has lived Lyotard's comment that "To reach the city centre, you must first go through the suburbs".[48]

2. The Order of Images

"Each time he walked past this enormous piece of furniture, he viewed it with satisfaction... It could be used for everything: it was memory, it was intelligence... No matter what one put inside it – once, a hundred times, ten thousand times – it was immediately retrievable, in the twinkling of an eye, so to speak. Forty-eight drawers! Enough space to store a whole world of well-ordered positive knowledge... 'The drawer', he sometimes said, 'is the foundation of the human mind.'"

Henri Bosco, *Monsieur Carré-Benoit à la campagne*[49]

At the end of the '50s, Paul Almasy's name was known all over: he had spent thirty years working as a journalist and twenty-five years as a photojournalist. *International Photography Year Book* ranked him alongside René Burri, Irving Penn, George Rodger and others as one of seven "Star Photographers" of 1960.

Students in front of the Sorbonne, 1968

Paul Almasy with his wife Elina, 1968

"Paul Almasy is seldom to be found at home in Paris. He is almost always on the road and seems to have been everywhere more than once... Almasy personifies author, photographer and researcher in one man...in Paul Almasy. He always knows exactly what he wants to say and what the best way is to tackle his article. But he also knows what pictures he needs which means he is able to work quite methodically... That he has been successful with this method is shown by the scope of his archives... When one considers that Almasy, besides travelling, photographing and taking notes, also writes the captions for each and every picture and also writes the finished articles to go with them, and, what's more, runs a successful picture agency, one begins to get an idea of the amount of work he puts in. Over and above this, he speaks seven languages fluently and writes with equal elegance in French and German."[50]

Burri, Penn and Rodger, besides Edouard Boubat, Henri Cartier-Bresson, Robert Doisneau and Willy Ronis are among the other French photographers who were introduced with a picture each in the 1960 *Year Book*, and are now names that have been known for decades in the world of photography. That Almasy's name is rather unfamiliar today, unlike in 1960, is the result of a unique development. "While modern art has eliminated the author, while structuralism has eliminated the subject, while the New Novel has eliminated the omnipresent narrator – at least in theory – the author in photography has been resurrected. The period since the '50s has been characterized by a growing perception of the photographer as an author", writes Urs Stahel of Winterthur Photography Museum, one of the outstanding centres of photography in Europe.[51] This development took place at a time of change in photojournalism: it was then starting to lose its dominance in journalistic reporting. "Photojournalism would take a back seat",[52] noted John Phillips, the first *LIFE* photographer for Europe and one of the Greats of his profession, even in the 1950s. "With TV's take-over of the news and the Leica's disappearance as the instrument of preference for the young man in search of truth," Jan-Erik Lundström wrote in *Real Stories*, "photojournalism began instead to claim the museum, the glossy coffee-table book, the art magazines, etc., for its existence."[53]

These developments passed Almasy by. He continued to travel the world non-stop and wrote articles, took photographs and filed them in his archives. "I am not a photographer, I am a photojournalist", Almasy claimed, but, to clarify his position, always liked to add: "I never specialized". This means that Almasy's name does not stand for a pre-selection of images selected by him, as is usual with photographers, but for the whole package. Paul Almasy devoted himself to the archive, to the order of pictures. It was in Paris, and since 1954 Neuilly, that the itinerant Almasy had his most important piece of furniture: an oak chest of drawers, eight drawers wide and a massive twenty drawers high. Each drawer was divided into three sections and could hold up to 1,200 negatives, each in its own envelope. The abbreviated names of different countries were written on the outside of the drawers. Almasy did not archive his black and white shots – an estimated 120,000 of them – according to when they were taken. He chose

instead to classify them by country; and each country had the same categories: history, state, political personalities, political events, economics, culture, sport, administration, army, education, transport, legal system, religion, health service, industry, agriculture, trade, the Arts, theatre, cinema, leisure time, music, folklore, the press, publishing houses, television, radio, housing, everyday life in the city, everyday life in the country, types of people, animals, plants, natural phenomena, shots of town and country, plus other subdivisions. It is an archive of the world in miniature, arranged with meticulous precision.

"At the peak of activity in the Neuilly period in the sixties, he had five full-time collaborators and one or two part-time. The archive people classified and added legends, retrieved pictures according to orders and received clients. In addition, the manual maintenance work was done by the same lady for more than twenty years: cutting and adapting the contact prints, matching each with its negative and glueing the print on a custom-made envelope containing the negative. Then each picture was numbered and placed in the files. The upkeep of the archive lists was made by Paul and his secretary. Paul also drew on each contact the cadrage he wanted for the enlargements",[54] recalled his wife Elina Almasy.

Before this native Norwegian and trained sociologist found a job in 1965, she helped out part-time in the office, raised the children, made lunch for the two or three others in the office and the family and saw to the mail in the evening. "From 1945–70, his secretary typed all his texts in French or in German that he dictated to her while marching up and down in the office. He usually only dictated in the afternoon, and sometimes went on until late in the evening when a story had to be delivered the next day. The copy was then language edited and corrected and retyped. Hard work in the days before electric typewriters and even computers! All mail was brought daily to the post-office, when it was not taken to the Gare de l'Est for the mail wagon of the train to Zurich. Later a special last-minute postal sorting centre for air-mail appeared."[55]

There is an essential difference between Almasy's approach and that of a photographer who takes on the role of author by making a distinction between the photographs that he authorizes and those he holds back. Almasy's starting point for most of his shots involves an unpretentious look at what he sees before him. This is how his great shots came about, apparently unintentionally, which only made them all the more effective, of course. What is characteristic of him is the attention he pays to the details within the whole picture. Whether it is the movement of people, animals or vehicles, landscape structures or urban setting, he often captures it all in what really is an incredible moment balanced between order and disorder. But the aesthetics of the 'decisive moment' are not his concern here. The compositional order of the shots that were taken and used for U.N. development projects represents his confident belief that the problems illustrated in the photographs can themselves be 'put in order', i.e. solved.

Almasy used to archive even his great shots among those from the same series that today seem much less impressive and he never stopped ordering his best shots in this way. Almasy's breadth and openness stand in contrast to the way many photographers insist on selecting and controlling their work, distilling it into a kind of poetry. His archive, negative archive and systematic catalogue in one also functioned in his absence. His presence was not essential if photographs had to be selected and interpreted and there is no one formula set in stone. Because his staff were familiar with the *Classement Almasy*, they were able to deal with publishers' and newspaper editors' requests for pictures and supply them. Many of Almasy's shots were often used long after they had been taken. Given his awareness of the world's problems and their priority, it is understandable that Almasy never made himself and his work the centre of attention as a system that lived off stars would have expected him to do. Almasy always photographed with his knowledge in the background or rather he photographed in a knowledgeable way that was to prompt the viewer into thinking about the background that had given rise to the image.

Almasy never devoted himself to aesthetic impressions. In his thinking, his writing and teaching, he distinguished sharply between "pictorial" and "functional" photography. He himself always viewed his work as "functional" photography and spoke out against the "annoying" tendency to "monopolize"[56] the term 'photography' as meaning only "pictorial" photography. Almasy never wore white gloves when handling his photographs and never made a fetish of photographs in the "white cube".[57] Aesthetics for him is only "a desirable added value, it's not essential".[58]

Almasy always worked with the written word and the image, as did the magazines in which he published, the illustrated newspapers of the '20s and '30s that "because of the way they communicate and the genres that are united in them, could be described as hybrid media".[59] There is no doubt that the 'career' enjoyed by the image was the more successful of the two in the twentieth century and led to a "hegemony of the image and its gradual supplanting of that of alphabetically organized documents".[60] "Photographic meaning depends largely on context", wrote Allan Sekula in "Reading an Archive", and:

"Meaning is always directed by layout, captions, text, and site and mode of presentation."[61]

If one of these aspects is disregarded, there is an imminent risk of aestheticism. "The very removal of these photographs from their initial contexts invites aestheticism",[62] noted Sekula in connection with another photography archive. "The new art history of photography at its too prevalent worst rummages through archives of every sort in search of masterpieces to celebrate and sell."[63] He considered instead "(moving) away from the art-historicist bias that governs most contemporary discussions of the medium. We need to understand how photography works within everyday life in advanced industrial societies: the problem is one of cultural history rather than art history."[64] "The archive has to be read from below, from a position of solidarity with those displaced, deformed, silenced,or made invisible by the machineries of profit and progress."[65]

In a tradition in which the artist is characterized by his originality, creativity and freedom, photography was long considered to be a mechanical medium for copyists and any activities involving organizing and classifying were always dismissed as inferior, as positivistic, bureaucratic pettiness.[66] In recent years and decades, the archive has been rehabilitated in a process started by Michel Foucault; indeed, more than that, it is now enjoying something of a boom and has almost become a trendy expression – especially when applied to the picture library. And now there is even talk of the 'art of archiving'.[67] Exhibitions like "Deep Storage, Collecting, Storing, and Archiving in Art"[68] show how many different artists are now creating archives, describe their work as archives or use archival strategies. In a move away from self-referral, the other common factor of '90s art has been its preoccupation with social issues or its involvement in social structures. The point is not that we have to recognize that even Almasy as an author in old-fashioned sense needs to be rehabilitated; rather the point is that he has side-stepped photographic developments in recent decades (outlined above) and is still with us – these days more than ever. "Fashions come and go, but the name of Almasy is destined to remain in the histories of photography", Edo Prando wrote in *Contemporary Photographers*.[69]

Anti-colonial graffiti in Algeria, 1963

Gypsy camp near Paris, 1969

La Défense, 1965

Almasy's work is unique: he has created a category of his own and his horizon is global in scope. He is the photographer of the modern age *par excellence*, not because his photographs were taken in the modern age, but because the structure of his work is formed by modernity. It is twentieth-century work in which twenty-first century problems already prefigured.

Finally, it is possibly still worth mentioning that Almasy recites polished anecdotes about many of the photographs he has taken the world over, but that when referring to his shots of Paris, his only comment is a curt "This is Paris". In all the publications about Paris in recent decades – "Paris, the City of Photographers"; "Paris, the Home of Photography" – Almasy has barely rated a mention. His only Paris publication in all that time has been a book wholly uncharacteristic of him, the photographer of the *condition humaine*, a small book of photos called *Eves de Paris*[70] that contains only shots of female statues.

It is thus not surprising – or maybe it is – that the line of Brassaï, André Kertész, Robert Doisneau, Edouard Boubat, Willy Ronis, Henri Cartier-Bresson and others is joined by Paul Almasy, a photographer of the city, with whom we can discover Paris or at least re-interpret it in the company of a man who saw the city from a different perspective.

1 Guillaume Apollinaire, *Zone* (Dublin 1972)
2 Paul Almasy, "Mon Crédo", p. 1.
3 Cf. Michel Butor, "Die Stadt als Text", in: Ursula Keller (Ed.), *Perspektiven metropolitaner Kultur* (Frankfurt/Main 2000)
4 Paul Almasy, "Ça c'est Paris!", (29), in German; the reportage number follows in brackets
5 Paul Almasy, "Dieser Mann will New York umbauen! Besuch im Atelier des berühmten Architekten Le Corbusier", (30), in German
6 Paul Almasy, *Exposition Mondiale, Paris,* (66), in German, 1937
7 Paul Almasy, "Nous voici dans l'ère des bidons/Im Zeichen des Benzin-Kanisters", (71), in French and German
8 Paul Almasy, "Menschen zwischen Sein und Nichtsein. Ein Blick in das Flüchtlings-Chaos von Paris / La France, Terre d'asile. Le flot des réfugiés continue d'arriver à Paris", (482), in French and German
9 Paul Almasy, "Zweite Heimat Paris. 'Pariserinnen aus fünf Erdteilen'", (731), in German
10 Cf. Saskia Sassen, *Migranten, Siedler, Flüchtlinge. Von der Massenauswanderung zur Festung Europa* (Frankfurt/Main 1996), pp. 8of, 82.
11 Ibid., p. 107.
12 Ibid., p. 103.
13 Paul Almasy, "La communité russe à Paris. Les réfugiés et leurs descandants", (Photo series FR[ANCE] 537)
14 Cf. Saskia Sassen, (see note 10), p. 95.
15 Ibid., pp. 107–108.
16 Paul Almasy, "Menschen zwischen Sein und Nichtsein. Ein Blick in das Flüchtlings-Chaos von Paris / La France, Terre d'asile. Le flot des réfugiés continue d'arriver à Paris", (482), in French and German
17 Cf. Saskia Sassen, ibid., p. 107
18 Paul Almasy, "Diese Menschen sind 'Schmuggelware'", (1303), in German, p. 2.
19 Ibid., p. 1.
20 Cf. Saskia Sassen, (see note 10), pp. 115/155.
21 Paul Almasy, "La Zône disparaît... / Elend verboten", (1133), in French and German, picture caption no. 2
22 Paul Almasy, "Allah in Paris. Der anhaltende Zustrom von Nordafrikanern bereitet der Bevölkerung und der Stadtverwaltung schwere Sorgen", (611), in German, p. 2.
23 Ibid., picture caption no. 14
24 Paul Almasy, "Mannequins", (622); "French Cancan", (975); "Tour Eiffel", (1036); "Eine Nacht im Quartier Latin", (1234); "Une nuit à Montmartre", (1238)
25 Paul Almasy, "Espions de la mode", (621)
26 Paul Almasy, "Jugend im Strome der Boulevards", (938), in German
27 Paul Almasy, "Blousons noirs", (1127), in French
28 Jean Paul Sartre, foreword in: Frantz Fanon, *The Wretched of the Earth* (New York 1963)
29 Ibid.
30 Ibid.
31 Paul Almasy, "Colons nord-africains", (893), in German and French
32 Cf. Saskia Sassen, (see note 10), pp. 115/155.
33 Frantz Fanon, *Black Skin, White Masks* (New York 1968)
34 Bernard Marrey, "Une volonté d'exclusion", in: Joseph Comby, Jacques Foucart, Bernard Marrey et al. (Eds.), *Paris perdu. Quarante ans de boueversement de la ville* (Paris 1995), p. 156.
35 Jean-François Lyotard, "Zone", in: Ursula Keller (Ed.), *Perspektiven metropolitaner Kultur* (Frankfurt/Main 2000), p. 119.
36 Paul Almasy, "Zigeuner soll kein Schimpfwort sein!", (1002), in German
37 Paul Almasy, "La Zône disparaît... / Elend verboten", (1133), in French and German, German picture caption no. 10.
38 Paul Almasy, "La plus gigantesque entreprise d'urbanisme du monde va commencer: Voici Paris de demain", (1180), in French
39 Jean-François Lyotard, (see note 35), p. 121.
40 Paul Almasy, "Villes artificielles, Nouvelles cités sans passé", (1189), in French
41 Jean-François Lyotard, (see note 35), p. 119.
42 Jean Baudrillard, "Die Stadt und der Haß", in: Ursula Keller (Ed.), *Perspektiven metropolitaner Kultur* (Frankfurt/Main 2000), pp. 130–141.
43 Cf. Pierre Bourdieu et al., *The Weight of the World: Social Suffering in Contemporary Society* (Stanford 1999)
44 Paul Almasy, "Paris change de peau", (1291), in French, picture caption no. 1
45 Ibid.
46 Philippe Vergne, "Avant-propos", in: Joseph Comby, Jacques Foucart, Bernard Marrey et al. (Eds.), *Paris perdu. Quarante ans de boueversement de la ville* (Paris 1995), p. 16.
47 Rem Koolhaas, "Fishing in Troubled Waters", in: C.C. Davidson (Ed.), *Anywise* (Cambridge 1996), pp. 157–162. Quoted here by Rem Koolhaas, "Asiatisch zu werden ist etwas sehr Radikales", in: Kai Vöckler und Dirk Luckow (Eds.) *Peking – Shanghai – Shenzen, Städte des 21. Jahrhunderts* (Frankfurt/Main, New York 2000), p. 442.
48 Jean-François Lyotard, (see note 35), p. 119.
49 Henri Bosco, *Monsieur Carré-Benoit à la campagne,* quoted in Gaston Bachelard, *The Poetics of Space* (New York 1964)
50 Norman Hall (Ed.), *International Photography Year Book* 1960 (London 1960), p.11f.
51 Urs Stahel, "Reportierende Fotografie und ihre Medien", in: Urs Stahel and Martin Gasser (Eds.), *Weltenblicke, Reportagefotografie und ihre Medien* (Zurich 1997), p. 16.
52 John Phillips, "About Photojournalism", in: John Phillips, *Free Spirit in a Troubled World* (Zurich, Berlin, New York 1996), p. 568.
53 Jan-Erik Lundström, "Real Stories", in: Jan-Erik Lundström, Finn Thrane, Helle Damsgård and Henning Hansen (Eds.), *Real Stories. Revisions in Documentary and Narrative Photography* (Odense), p. 4.
54 Fax from Elina Almasy to the author, 14.04.2001
55 Ibid.
56 Paul Almasy, "Mon Crédo", in French, p. 1
57 Cf. Brian O'Doherty, *Inside the White Cube, The Ideology of the Gallery Space* (Berkeley 1999)
58 Almasy, (see note 56), p. 3.
59 Peter M. Spangenberg, "... and my Eyes are only Holograms". "Formen operierender Kontingenz in hybriden Medien", in: Irmela Schneider, Christian W. Thomson (Eds.), *Hybridkultur: Medien, Netze, Künste* (Cologne 1997), p. 142.
60 Sanford Kwinter, Daniela Fabricius, "Urbanism: An Archivist's Art", in: Francine Ford, Michel Jacques (Eds.), *Mutations* (Bordeaux 2000), pp. 494–503.
61 Allan Sekula, "Reading an Archive", in: Brian Wallis (Ed.), *Blasted Allegories. An Anthology of Writings by Contemporary Artists* (Cambridge 1989), p. 117.
62 Allan Sekula, p. 123.
63 Ibid., p. 117f.
64 Ibid., p. 125.
65 Ibid., p. 127.
66 Ibid., pp. 119/123.
67 Cf. Geoffrey Batchen, "The Art of Archiving", in: Ingrid Schaffner, Matthias Winzen, *Deep Storage, Collecting, Storing, and Archiving in Art* (Munich, New York 1998), pp. 46–60.
68 Ingrid Schaffner, Matthias Winzen, *Deep Storage, Collecting, Storing, and Archiving in Art* (Munich, New York 1997)
69 Edo Prando, "Paul Almasy", in Colin Naylor (Ed.), *Contemporary Photographers* (Chicago, London 1988), p. 18.
70 Paul Almasy, *Eves de Paris* (Veviers, Paris 1964)

Plates

Empty frames in the Louvre during wartime, 1940s

German troops arriving in Paris, 1940

Celebrating peace, 1945

"I've just come from Auschwitz –
I'm the only survivor from 1000", 1945

Museum attendant in front of a Charles de Gaulle poster, ca. 1945

Election day, 1945

Charles de Gaulle at a press conference, 1958

Street trader at the entrance to the metro, 1937

TV reporters at a NATO conference, 1960

Street musician in the Jewish quarter, 1947

The departure of emigrants from
the Saint Lazare railway station, 1947

Bistro talk, 1953

Lovers at the bar, 1961

Couple at a café, 1966

Colette in her apartment at
the Palais Royal, 1946

Jaques Prévert, 1957

Léonor Fini with her cats, 1958

Jean Cocteau drawing a portrait
of Maria Calvi, 1958

Alberto Giacometti working on a sculpture, 1960

Alberto Giacometti in his favourite café, 1960

Alberto Giacometti in front of his
studio, 1960

Serge Gainsbourg playing pinball, 1959

Talking cab drivers, 1956

A happy moment, 1952

Little girl on a tricycle-horse, 1956

Cycling in Paris, 1948

Traffic at the Place St-Augustin, 1948

Nuns in a courtyard, 1952

"Just need five Francs for a *pipo*", 1947

Young boy reading the newspaper, 1947

In the Jardin du
Luxembourg, 1945

At school, ca. 1960

Streetlife, 1952

Steps to Montmartre, 1960s

Along the Seine, 1960s

Relaxing at the Seine, 1960s

Rock 'n' roll on the banks of the Seine, 1950s

Dancing, ca. 1960

In front of a club, ca. 1960

Lovers, 1948

For Immediate Release
Contact: Madeline Schwarz
mschwarz@prestel-usa.com
Tel: (212) 995-2720, Ext. 24
Fax: (212) 995-2733

Paul Almasy
Paris

By Klaus Kleinschmidt and Axel Schmidt

For centuries, Paris has been a home and inspiration to artists, writers, and musicians. In the twentieth century the French capital served as host and subject to some of the greatest names in photography, including Eugene Atget, Robert Doisneau, and Henri Cartier-Bresson. In his new book *Paul Almasy: Paris*, another photographer takes his place in this tradition as seen through eighty-one stunning duotone images of the city.

Born in Budapest in 1906, Paul Almasy left Hungary at the age of eighteen to pursue a career as a photojournalist. He spent the next fifty years circling the globe and chronicling some of the greatest events and people of the time. With the liberation of Paris and the end of World War II Almasy made his home in the French capital. *Paul Almasy: Paris* collects Almasy's photographs from the German occupation to the end of the 1960s, depicting a compelling mix of everyday street scenes, important public events, and portraits of the city's most prominent denizens.

Almasy captures the elusive character of the real Paris, for the most part hidden from tourists and disappearing as the French capital became an international metropolis. His photographs observe Parisian life along the Seine: dances performed along its banks, a solitary figure walking among the river's barges and bathers enjoying the sun at a public pool. He takes the viewer into the back streets and alleyways, stealing glimpses at the street musicians, lovers in bars, friends at bistros and cafes and patrons outside of clubs.

As a photographer of high standing, Almasy had access to the political and cultural elite of Paris. The book includes photographs of writers, artists, and leading politicians. There are portraits, among others, of Colette and Andre Breton, Yves Saint Laurent, Man Ray and Alberto Giacometti, Charles de Gaulle and Dwight D. Eisenhower.

In marked contrast to these photographs taken in the halls of power and influence, the book presents Almasy's compassionate images of the city's dispossessed. Almasy was concerned with the plight of the city's gypsies and there are pictures of a gypsy baptism, a gypsy camp, a woman filling a watering can, and a young brother and sister walking hand-in-hand. The book also includes Almasy's photographs of an Auschwitz survivor, France's migrant workers, and the city's homeless. Interspersed with these often intimate photographs are Almasy's images of great historical events: German troops arriving in the city, Parisians celebrating the end of World War II and the funeral at Paul Valéry.

175 Fifth Avenue, Suite 402, New York, NY 10010 *telephone:* (212) 995-2720 *facsimile:* (212) 995-2733
www.prestel.com

Now in his tenth decade, Almasy lives outside Paris and devotes a great deal of time to maintaining his extensive photographic archive. Estimated at more than 120,000 images, Almasy's work is a testament to the photographer's remarkable near century-long career. *Paul Almasy: Paris* provides a telling portrait of the great city, the public and the personal, as lived during the middle part of the twentieth century.

About the Publisher:
Founded in 1924 and with over 300 English titles in print, Prestel publishes fine books on art, architecture, and photography, and has offices in Munich, London, and New York.

About the Book:

Title:	Paul Almasy: Paris
Authors	Klaus Kleinschmidt and Axel Schmidt
ISBN:	3-7913-2597-3
Price:	$39.95
Pages:	96
Illustrations:	69 duotone and 12 b&w illustrations
Trim size:	9 ½ x 11 ¼ inches
Pub Date:	November 2001

Please send two tearsheets upon review.

Couples in front of a dancing hall, 1950s

Gypsy baptism, ca. 1950

Gypsy camp, ca. 1950

Illegal Portuguese immigrants setting up home, 1963

The making of mannequins, 1948

Gypsy woman, 1949

Brother and sister, 1953

Two men and a dog, 1958

Backyard in Ménilmoutant, 1950s

The *Blousons Noirs* on the road, 1965

A young couple, 1960

On the Champs-Elysées, 1947

Barges on the Seine, 1950

Les Halles, 1950

A blind beggar, ca. 1950

Sleeping in doorways, 1962

Steps to Montmartre, 1947

Chez Nadia, 1960

In the Jewish quarter, 1962

Painting a lantern pole, 1950s

Waiting at a bus stop, 1967

Cleaning up under the Eiffel Tower, 1952

Cheese transport, 1960

Butcher at Les Halles, 1950s

End of the shift at the Renault factory, 1954

Georges Mathieu, 1964

Poster billing, 1952

Cancan at the Tabarin, 1957

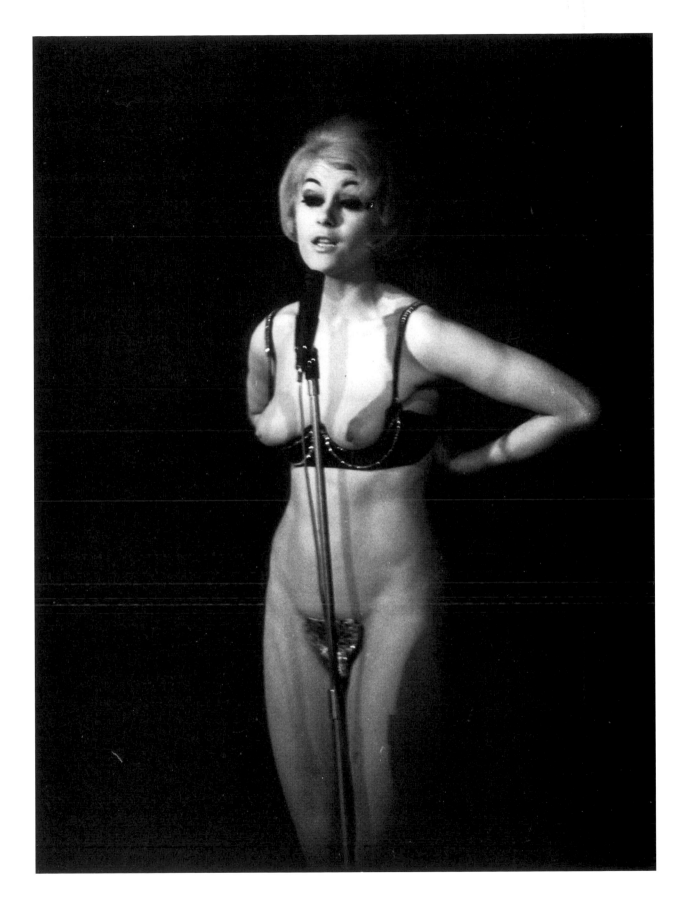

Striptease, 1962

A dinner at the Elysée Palace, 1955

Romy Schneider and Alain Delon, 1963

The Duke of Windsor at a
gala dinner at the Lido, 1960

André Breton, 1960

Léopold and Germain Survage in the painter's studio, 1950

Man Ray in his studio, 1960

Yves Saint Laurent, 1961

The funeral of Paul Valéry, 1945

View of the Place de la Concorde at night, 1960

Onlookers, 1955

Stockbrokers, 1950

A public pool on the Seine, 1964

Winter scene in the Jardin des Tuileries, 1968

Clearing snow in the Jardin du Luxembourg, 1968

Paris 12.672 km, Vietnam, 1950

Biography

1906
Born in Budapest, May 29th

1924–28
Studied political science in Vienna, Munich and Heidelberg

1929–31
Correspondent for the German press agency Wehr, in Rome

1932–34
Reportages from various European countries

1935
Started photographing on a journey around South America. Photographic reportage for the *Berliner Illustrirte Zeitung* on the Finnish team's preparations for the Winter Olympic Games

1936
Crossed the Sahara by car for the *Berliner Illustrirte Zeitung*

1938
Accredited as Swiss correspondent by the French government

1940–43
Reported from Germany, France, Belgium and The Netherlands with the permission of the German Army

1944–51
Reportages from Europe, the Middle East, Asia, Africa and Australia

1952
Worked for the international U.N. organizations: UNESCO, UNICEF, WHO, IAO and FAO,

1955
Photographed artists Bernard Buffet, Jean Cocteau, Alexandre Calder, Alberto Giacometti, etc.

1956
He founded the organization Gens d'Images, with Albert Plécy

1957–71
Reportages from all the world's continants

1972–89
Taught at several universities: Centre de Perfectionnement des Journalistes, Paris; Ecole Technique de la Photographie et de l'Audiovisuel, Toulouse; CESLA (Centre d'Etudes des Lettres et des Sciences Appliqués), at the Sorbonne in Paris; Ecole Supérieure de Journalisme, Lille; CIM (Centre d'Information sur les Médias), Ecole Technique de la Photographie et de l'Audiovisuel, Rennes

1993
Knight of the French 'Ordre du Mérite'

Paul Almasy lives near Paris